THE
BLUEPRINT
TO BUILDING CLIENTELE

THE FOUNDATION AND PRACTICE TO BUILDING AND MAINTAINING A CONSISTENT CLIENTELE

BY
LARISSA LANE

Manufactured in the United States of America

www.LarissaLane.com

ISBN-13:978-1979098809
ISBN-10:1979098808

DEDICATION

I want to dedicate this BLUEPRINT to those of you in the industry serving customers. This is to those whom have the desire to better themselves in business and for personal use. When you learn information, you should share the information you learned to help others. I would also like to dedicate this to my father and mother, Lamont and Samantha Lane, and to my mentor Chelsea Glover for displaying your Blueprint of what hard work and dedication looks like.

THIS BLUEPRINT BELONGS TO

DATE STARTED

CONTENTS

Introduction	7
Branding	11
Schedule Availability	19
Client Retention	21
Pricing. Discounting. Incentives.	27
Client Consistency & Intentional Goal Setting	33
Networking	41
Advertising & Marketing	47
Professionalism & Etiquette	51
Building Techniques	55
Final Thoughts	63
Acknowledgment	64
Meet the Author	65

INTRODUCTION

I graduated beauty school in 2009 with the hopes of working in a salon and making lots of money, I knew I would have to work hard to get what I wanted but I never thought I would have to work this hard. I thought I would have to work hard at styling hair. In fact, I thought if I styled hair well, clients would flock to me. Oh, how wrong I was! In beauty school, they didn't focus much on how to get clients in the door, only the basics of cosmetology. However, in today's world, being a stylist is running your own business. I worked in a salon as an assistant before but then I decided since I was licensed it was time to do my own thing, I worked at home as a stylist for a little while, however I became uncomfortable with people and different energy being in my house. I randomly started working in another salon that was commission based so my paycheck would be inconsistently fluctuating. I remember my first check was $44 after taxes were taken, I was so angry. This approach wasn't going to work for me so I got a second job because I wasn't giving up my dream as a hairstylist. After working a year, my paycheck in the salon only reached a minimum wage average for two weeks, but still inconsistent and not enough money to live on. I started paying attention to fluctuating times. Clientele was low in the early winter and late summer time due to the upcoming holidays and clients going on vacations. I could keep track of the schedule and budget correctly. As another year passed I noticed my check start averaging a little more for two weeks. Even with the increase it still was not enough for me, and I was determined to change something. I came up with a plan for myself and stayed consistent with this plan for a year to see what happened.

Next thing I knew my check was averaging almost double the amount every two weeks. After following the plan year after year and seeing my checks continue to increase, I had discovered a plan that works. At one point, I thought, hey maybe this increase is luck so I stopped for a few months, and my checks started to decrease. I decided that it was not luck; it was the fact that I made the choice to put in the work to make sure I succeed in this business as a stylist. I learned a lot along this journey, and I hope you get out of it what I have. I present to you the BLUEPRINT to BUILDING Clientele Manual and Workbook.

I
AM
MY
BRAND

BRANDING

- Your brand is your promise to your customer. It tells them what they can expect from your products and services and how it differentiates from other products and services.
- You are your own BRAND!
- You are the representation of your brand and so are your clients. How you present yourself is what your brand is saying.
- You need to become the expert on what you are representing. Research and attend classes on the services or products you are giving or distributing.
- You need to make your presence known. Make sure there is a direct correlation between what you are offering either individually or as a company. People will start to become familiar of your brand where ever you go.
- You need to utilize others to further promote you brand: friends, family members, and associates can all be supporting and promoting your brand.

Define your BRAND and what it offers

_____

_____

What do you do?

_____

_____

What do you want to represent?

_____

_____

How does your brand compliment your services?

_____

_____

Where do you want your brand to be recognized?

_____

_____

What do you want people to think when they see your brand/ logo?

_____

_____

What are you good at? (your Niche)

_____

_____

What sets you apart from the products or services of your competitors?

_____

_____

Define your goals & objectives

List five of your goals?

1.

2.

3.

4.

5.

Manage your brand (YOU). You should spend an hour or more a day managing your brand and making sure its running the way you want it to. If it is not, then you should make corrections. If you're are working for someone for hours out of a day and helping his/her dreams excel, then you should be able to work for yourself for at least an hour.

Everything should be in sync: Social Media, Website, email, related material you produce. Whatever you are posting about your business should be the same. What your ad looks like on social media should coincide across all platforms. What is on your website or your posters and even your business cards.

Set aside daily and weekly time to manage your brand. This activity should become a daily routine to you.

*PUT YOUR BEST FOOT FORWARD
Listen to what people say- make sure the look, perception, and personality of your brand lines up with how, you want consumers and clients to speak of you

Your Goals & Objectives
Set S.M.A.R.T goals meaning each goal should be Specific. Measureable. Achievable. Relevant. Timely. Below list five goals and your objectives.

1. Goal: _____

   Objective: _____

   Specific: _____

   Measureable: _____

   Achievable: _____

   Relevant: _____

   Timely: _____

2. Goal: _____

   Objective: _____

   Specific: _____

   Measureable: _____

   Achievable: _____

   Relevant: _____

   Timely: _____

3. Goal: _____

   Objective: _____

   Specific: _____

   Measureable: _____

   Achievable: _____

   Relevant: _____

   Timely: _____

4. Goal: _____

   Objective: _____

   Specific: _____

   Measureable: _____

   Achievable: _____

   Relevant: _____

   Timely: _____

5. Goal: _____

   Objective: _____

   Specific: _____

   Measureable: _____

   Achievable: _____

   Relevant: _____

   Timely: _____

NOTHING CAN STOP GODS PLAN FOR ME

SCHEDULE AVAILABILITY

When deciding what your schedule looks like, you need to make sure you are available during your scheduled times. If you have scheduled yourself to work make sure that you are working. If a client wants to come in during that time and you are not in the salon, you need to be available to take the appointment. Your calendar should have all the days you plan not to work for the year, ex: Holidays, Birthdays, Anniversary's, Vacations.
*Note: Emergencies happen and we occasionally get sick, those are things we have no control over.

What's your availability?

Days:	S	M	T	W	T	F	S
Times/ Hours:							

Ensure your clients know when you have available appointments. Send out an email blast or a social media post to inform them. You should not leave it up to the salons to do all your client scheduling. Be aware of how your being scheduled and make sure your also scheduling clients.

A GOAL WITHOUT A PLAN IS JUST A WISH

-Antoine de Saint- Exupéry

CLIENT RETENTION

- Communication is key. You cannot create loyalty if your clients are not paying attention to you
- Be sure you give your client a thorough consultation to help prevent miscommunication (see perfect consultation figure 1)
- Stand for something (hair care, wonderful customer service, good lifestyle, positivity)

What makes you great?

_____

_____

- Be honest with your clients. If you cannot provide a certain service or its uncomfortable, tell the client that you don't perform that service and then recommend someone you know who may. *Looks good on you in the client's eyes and in the person, you recommended*
- Stay positive in your communication around your client. (ex. Gossiping about your peers or people is a no go, you are supposed to uplift your clients and gossiping looks like you can't be trusted)?
- Conversation Ideas (hair, family, movies, upcoming events, music, good news, products, hair care, summer vacations, magazines, school, etc.)
- Educate them on hair products and services: You need to teach them how to care for their hair, hairstyle, and the products you recommend for them
- Go above the client expectations and offer them bottle water, coffee, tea, or wine. If it's raining and they don't have an umbrella, walk them to their car.
- Most clients prefer quality over quantity regarding service.

Make sure you are not over booking yourself. Practice your time management and keep track so you don't have clients waiting all day to be serviced. If you are running behind, contact your next client and let them know. Give them the option to reschedule. When scheduling your color appointments or any other lengthy appointments, inform your clients of that possibility and they should make arrangements in case they are being serviced longer than expected.

****You are the PROFESSIONAL****

BHbL Consultation (figure 1)

BHbL (Beautiful Hair by Larissa) Consultation

I'm going to ask you a few questions about your hair
1. How would you rate your hair condition 1-10?
2. Rate your current hairstyle 1-10
3. Rate your color 1-10
4. Do you have any allergies? If yes, what are they?
5. What are your current products your using at home? Rate them 1-10
6. What are your current styling tools? Rate them 1-10
7. What are your challenges and concerns with your hair?
8. On a scale of 1-10, how committed are you to addressing these concerns?
9. What is your hair goal?
10. What do you love about your hair?
11. What do you do daily with your hair?
12. How active are you? Do you sweat a lot?
13. Are you able to duplicate your hairstyles at home? What could help you in that?
14. How often do you want to deal with your hair?
15. Do you prefer your hair in/ out of your face?
16. What would make your hair experience a 10 today?
17. Rate your personal style with 1 being polished and neat 10 being wild and edgy
18. How did you hear about us?

Consultation

Below list 10 additional questions of your own, pertaining to your career.

1.

2.

3.

4.

5.

6.

7.

8.

9.

10.

LIVE EVERYDAY WITH INTENTION

PUSH YOURSELF EVEN WHEN YOU DON'T WANT TO

-Larissa Lane

PRICING. DISCOUNTS. INCENTIVES.

Pricing should coincide with your market and skill level. Do not over or out price yourself, or clients may never sit in your chair. If you are providing a discount to new clients, current clients, friends, and family members all the time, keep in mind that it does not look good for your business unless that is the culture of your business/brand. When you choose to constantly discount prices for your services, you are only asking for bargain shoppers, and it becomes an expectation. Bargain shoppers only go where the deals are. They don't stay when deals end. Look at it like this, how many deals and discounts do you get when you go to the doctor's office or the dentist or high-end stores?

Current client discounts are appropriate for birthdays, holidays, anniversary's, and Client Appreciation Week, reward your current clients. It's unfair to reward individuals who are not your current clients. Giving incentives to clients to help bring new clients like a referral program is an option, for example every number of clients they refer, they may receive a percentage off or a complimentary service.

The clients you receive from discounted services will not be permanent clients so be intentional about not cheating yourself.

***Go easy on discounting services, it's bad for business and your image**

Pricelist
Below list your services offered and your prices across or next to them.

Ex. **Styling**
- Shampoo style — $45
- Up-do/ Up-style — $65+
- Reshaping/ Cut — $35

Waxing
- Underarm — $35
- Bikini — $45

Hair color
- Highlighting — $55+
- Single Process — $50+

Discounts

On the table below you're going to create your own discounts for which ever months of your choosing.

*Go easy on discounting.

MONTH/ YEAR	SERVICE TO BE DISCOUNTED	DESCRIPTION
Ex: September 2017	All color services	30% off all color services with the purchase of a blowout

MONTH/ YEAR	SERVICE TO BE DISCOUNTED	DESCRIPTION

Incentives
Below list 5 additional incentives for your clients.

Ex: Every five clients you recommend that receives a service, you get 55% off your next styling service.

1.

2.

3.

4.

5.

CONSISTENCY IS KEY

CLIENT CONSISTENCY & INTENTIONAL GOAL SETTING

Consistent stylist attracts consistent clients.
- Be consistently intentional about your goals, success happens. When you are booking clients, and managing your schedule be mindful. If your schedule is slow go back and see who is missing, who has not been in your chair in a while, give them a call and get them back in your chair
- Pay attention to how many clients you have a week/day compared to how many you want to have.
- Rebook clients and make sure they book for the year. The importance of rebooking is to assure your client that they will be able to get in even when you get booked up. Rebooking also benefits you. By booking for the year you will be able to gauge how much money you will make and you create consistency.

WHY IS PRE-BOOKING IMPORTANT TO YOU?

_____

_____

How many clients do you have in a Week? _____

Day? _____

How many you want to have a Week? _____

Day? _____

*Utilize your contact list (cell phone, email, social media)

How many of them are your clients? _____

GET THEM IN YOUR CHAIR
Set client goals, for example, if your goal is *I want to have 7 clients a day.*
 Do everything you can think of to meet that goal or ask a friend or associate to help you.

Let's put everything in to action. On the grid let's intentionally set your goals and make a habit out of it. Remember you benefit from what how much work you put in.

Intentional Goal Setting

Date

	S	M	T	W	T	F	S
How many clients scheduled							
How many clients arrived							
How many clients no showed							
How many clients rescheduled							
How many clients did you call to come in							

What were your strengths this week?

What were your weaknesses this week?

How will you improve for next week?

Intentional Goal Setting

Date

	S	M	T	W	T	F	S
How many clients scheduled							
How many clients arrived							
How many clients no showed							
How many clients rescheduled							
How many clients did you call to come in							

What were your strengths this week?

What were your weaknesses this week?

How will you improve for next week?

Intentional Goal Setting

Date

	S	M	T	W	T	F	S
How many clients scheduled							
How many clients arrived							
How many clients no showed							
How many clients rescheduled							
How many clients did you call to come in							

What were your strengths this week?

What were your weaknesses this week?

How will you improve for next week?

Intentional Goal Setting

Date

	S	M	T	W	T	F	S
How many clients scheduled							
How many clients arrived							
How many clients no showed							
How many clients rescheduled							
How many clients did you call to come in							

What were your strengths this week?

What were your weaknesses this week?

How will you improve for next week?

I BELIEVE IN MYSELF, I AM UN-STOPPABLE

BE ORIGINAL. BE YOU.

NETWORKING

The Key point of networking events is to meet new people and build relationships, not to hang out with your current friends.

- Be Social; remember to put your phone down and socialize. Attend networking events by yourself or with one additional person (the social butterfly). The point of bringing an addition social friend with you is if you're not the socialite, you're learning how to become social

***You become who you surround yourself with**

- Always carry business cards with you that has current information available. What is the point of having a business card with information on it if no one can reach you? Having a business card with updated information on it also makes you look professional.
- Introduce yourself with confidence (Hello/ Hi my name is _____. I am a _____, how are you? What's your name? or Sorry, I didn't catch your name)

***Try not to force conversation; let it flow naturally**

- Most people are socially awkward because they don't know what to say or what to talk about, so here are a few topics for you to keep in mind.

Networking topics:
- Current event (How did they hear about it? How the event is going?)
- Take interest in their career or workplace
- Upcoming events happening
- Restaurants, etc. (light conversation in case a fellow networker wanted to join in)

*Google networking topic for more conversation pieces.
When conversing with fellow networkers be sure not to make promises you can't keep or don't intend to keep with new people.
ex. I'll give you a call so we can do lunch.
It is ok to say it was nice meeting you and then you move on to next person.
RELAX & ENJOY YOURSELF

My Network
Below you are going to keep track of your network.

Date

Networking Event

Who did you meet new?

Do you plan to stay connected to them?

How do you plan to stay connected to them?

What can you do better at next time?

Date

Networking Event

Who did you meet new?

Do you plan to stay connected to them?

How do you plan to stay connected to them?

What can you do better at next time?

Date

Networking Event

Who did you meet new?

Do you plan to stay connected to them?

How do you plan to stay connected to them?

What can you do better at next time?

Date

Networking Event

Who did you meet new?

Do you plan to stay connected to them?

How do you plan to stay connected to them?

What can you do better at next time?

My Surroundings
You're the average of the five people you spend the most time with. The ones you spend most of your time with tells a lot about the person you are and the way you think. The more positivity you would like to come your way, the more positivity you need to surround yourself with. If a healthier lifestyle is something you want to embrace, you should surround yourself around like-minded people. If growing your business is what you want to do, then you need to surround yourself around people who are doing just that. It's not that you can't be friends or engage with those you may currently be around, it's just that people who are not helping you move to the next level can be a distraction. Friends and family who are for you and love you will understand when you are trying to grow. For those who don't may have just been in your life for a season or two. Below you're going to fill out who you are surrounded by and why your around them. Then you're going to fill out who you want to be surrounded by and why you want to be around them.

The people I engage with and why

1.

2.

3.

4.

5.

The people I want to engage with and why

1.

2.

3.

4.

5.

ADVERTISING/ MARKETING

In today's media environment, we have so many resources at our disposal to advertise and market ourselves and a lot of it is free. Marketing and Advertising are like each other but not the exact same, many people confuse the two. Marketing is the communication between your brand and the target audience (the community you want to attract). Advertising is a form of marketing communication used to promote or sell your services and products.

- Social Media plays a large role in advertising, but you shouldn't limit yourself to it.

Social Media examples: Instagram, Facebook, Periscope, Twitter, You Tube, LinkedIn, Snap Chat, Facebook Live (see figure 2)

BE CONSISTENT

- Create Website/ Landing page (Branding) it shows your work and you look professional

Your clients are walking advertisement for you. Utilize them as much as possible.

- If you do events as a vendor, get the information of anyone that comes to you so you can keep in contact ex. Name, number, email, social media, address

Join appropriate online/ local communities, ex. hairstylist groups, nail groups, local spa groups.

Marketing Questionnaire

What does your normal client look like?

_____

What type of clients do you want to attract?

_____

What age group do you want to service?

_____

_____

What type of places do your client shop?

_____

_____

What type of career does your client have?

_____

_____

Whom are your services offered to?

_____

_____

_____

Advertising
Social media post should be to the point (Short & Sweet)
Newspaper
Radio advertisement
Radio or social media interview
Email
Networking
Newsletter
Be active in the community
Car door magnet
Product labels
T-shirts
Business cards
Post cards
Coffee mugs
Tote bags
Banners
Window decal

(Figure 2)
example of an advertising Post

NOW BOOKING
347.719.BHbL(2425)
LarissaLane1@gmail.com

> BEING POSITIVE IN A NEGATIVE SITUATION IS NOT NAÏVE. ITS LEADERSHIP
>
> -Ralph Marston

PROFESSIONALISM/ ETIQUETTE

Professionalism and etiquette are signs of your character.

If you work in a salon you should abide by the salon rules even if others are not. This behavior is what separates you from them. Your goal is to always act professional. How you treat people reflects who you are. The rules of the industry you are working in also includes the way you dress. It is always positive to dress in your own style however it should always look and smell clean. Your attire should be in line with the salon/ industry guidelines, the safe way to go is without showing the 3B's (No belly's, No booty's, or No boobs) unless that's the culture of the salon/ industry.

Pay attention to your language in front of your clients, everyone is listening (all conversations are not meant for the salon). Do not speak badly about any one, especially the people you work with or other clients because gossip is bad for business and you look untrustworthy.

Personal calls on your cellphone are inappropriate and make your day longer (if it's important have them call the business phone unless your business phone is your cell phone).

Punctuality is crucial to success. Punctuality as a stylist, I understand that is hard, but TIME IS MONEY. Keep in mind that your clients have other things to do; respect your clients time, and they will respect yours.

    *Be professional, NO EXCUSES**

Rules & Regulations
Below create a few of your own rules and regulations to follow.

1. _____

2. _____

3. _____

4. _____

5. _____

6. _____

7. _____

8. _____

9. _____

10. _____

MY ATTITUDE DETERMINES MY DIRECTION

LIFE IS ONLY AS GOOD AS YOUR MINDSET

BUILDING TECHNIQUES

Invest in yourself

"Investing in yourself is the best thing you can do. Anything that improves your own talents; nobody can tax or take it away from you. They can run up huge deficits and the dollar can be worth far less. You can have all kinds of things happen. But if you've got talent yourself, and you've maximized your talent, you've got a tremendous asset that can return ten-fold."
-WARREN BUFFETT

Continue to attend classes for techniques, industry knowledge, and financial intelligence
Practice. Practice. Practice your craft and post your work. Pick at least two people and practice on the them, then post pictures of your work. People need to see what you can do to trust you.
Work on becoming a better person… WHY?
Most people think being skilled is what keeps clients, that is false. Would you continue to be serviced by someone who's work was amazing but their attitude sucked? Clients stay because they like you, they like your conversation, they like your energy, and they trust you.
People like the way you make them look, however they love the way you make them feel!
Reading books to help elevate you and your mindset also helps your outlook on life. The energy you put in to the atmosphere is the energy you get back, I like to look at it as if I am going to benefit double time the hard work I put in. I also pray a lot and keep God first in everything I do, because at the end of the day it's him that give us extra strength to be better. I recommended a few books to read that helped me along my way that I'm sure will help elevate you and your success as well.

Book List Recommendation
Rich Dad Poor Dad by Robert Kiyosaki
The Secret to Success by Eric Thomas
The Choice is Yours by John C. Maxwell
Secrets of the World Class by Steve Siebold
The Ant and the Elephant by Vince Poscente

Building Techniques

Let's create your own building techniques!

What are techniques you want to build on?

1.

2.

3.

Classes you would like to attend?	Date	What is your plan to get there?	Did I attend?

Things you want to let go	When are you letting them go?

Books to read	Date Started	Date Finished

Affirmations

Affirmations are the actions of a process. Creating affirmations can be emotionally supportive to some. It takes twenty-one days to create a habit, you have twenty-three days of affirmations to help guide you to a new mindset.

List daily affirmations:

Date:
Affirmation:

Date:
Affirmation:

Date:
Affirmation:

Date:
Affirmation:

Date:
Affirmation:

Date:
Affirmation:

Date:
Affirmation:

Date:
Affirmation:

Date:
Affirmation:

Date:
Affirmation:

Date:
Affirmation:

Date:
Affirmation:

Date:
Affirmation:

Date:
Affirmation:

Date:
Affirmation:

Date:
Affirmation:

Date:
Affirmation:

Date:
Affirmation:

Date:
Affirmation:

Date:
Affirmation:

Date:
Affirmation:

Date:
Affirmation:

Date:
Affirmation:

FINAL THOUGHTS

This plan has helped me in the most wonderful way and I know it will be beneficial to you as well. I'm not saying it's a perfect plan because nothing is perfect. I pray you get from this what is necessary for you. You should be proud of yourself for taking the first step in purchasing the Blueprint to Building Clientele. I am happy for you and proud of you for having the drive. Creating this project has had many obstacles, however trusting God in every step of the way has fine-tuned this project to be such a masterpiece. This is just the beginning, continue to grow. There will be a lot of ups and downs in whatever industry you're in, you have to keep going. Don't give up, even on those hard days. Just do it, and be the best you know how to be while doing so. Great things are already within you, keep your drive and ambition and there is no limit to how far and how high you can go. Let God guide you through your journey and allow you to create your Blueprint for someone else. Keep going, you got this.

ACKNOWLEDGEMENT

Thank you to God, this is your vision and I'm just following your guidance. To my mother and father, thank you for loving me and allowing me to grow in my own way. Thank you for showing me and being an example of what drive and hard work is. Brittney, my sister and best friend, I appreciate your honesty all the time and keeping me honest. Thank you for learning to support my goals and my journey. Gary Brown, thank you for being a huge portion of my life, thank you for your continuous love and support. Thank you for your push in helping me kick starting my journey my journey in the beauty industry when no one else would and supporting it over the years. Chelsea Glover, thank you for your guidance, thank you for providing your time and love to pour into me as much as you have and grooming me for this profession and my personal life. Thank you for providing a mentally and physically stabled place for the Blueprint to be built, you are and will always be a one of a kind mentor and big sister. My best friends, Winter and Cameron Clay, thank you for pushing me to be greater and challenging me to go after my goals. Deaja Vire and Tionna (T-BAEbee) Brisker, thank you for being my business partners and my friends, you have both supported me in this project since I mentioned it to you. Ms. Nicole Berry, the greatest business coach I could have ever asked for. Thank you for being supportive, positive and a role model for me. You are truly a gift from God. Thank you to my beautiful clients; my celebrities, without you ladies, none of this would have been possible. You are all phenomenal women and I couldn't thank God for better clients. Thank you all for sticking with me and my goofy self. Thank you Maggie Kniola for your help in my editing process, and thank you Aliyan Mughal and Tamika Cotton for your graphic design services while bringing this vision into fruition.

MEET THE AUTHOR

Larissa Lane, an innovative hair artist, Cosmetology Educator, and constant student to her industry, is a vibrant woman who consistently inspires and motivates those she comes into contact with. As a proud entrepreneur and business owner for 10 years, Larissa has dedicated her focus to take branding and marketing to new levels. Being a creative thinker has kept her consistently finding new and better ways to keep her clientele happy and educated. Larissa is always determined to give back to the beauty industry and to those she meets in the midst of her journey. She is personable, meticulous, talented, chic and ambitious. Larissa goes after what she believes, allowing nothing and no one to deter her. She is passionate about what she does. Her professionalism and expertise shine through her work. She is an amazing stylist and motivator of others who cares about you and your hair in the most genuine way.

www.ingramcontent.com/pod-product-compliance
Lightning Source LLC
Chambersburg PA
CBHW040324220526
45473CB00009B/2553